EARTH SCIENCE FAIR PROJECTS

JORDAN MCGILL

www.av2books.com

Go to www.av2books.com, and enter this book's unique code.

BOOK CODE

V445837

AV² by Weigl brings you media enhanced books that support active learning.

AV² provides enriched content that supplements and complements this book. Weigl's AV² books strive to create inspired learning and engage young minds in a total learning experience.

Your AV² Media Enhanced books come alive with...

Audio
Listen to sections of the book read aloud.

Key Words
Study vocabulary, and complete a matching word activity.

Video
Watch informative video clips.

Quizzes
Test your knowledge.

Embedded Weblinks
Gain additional information for research.

Slide Show
View images and captions, and prepare a presentation.

Try This!
Complete activities and hands-on experiments.

... and much, much more!

Published by AV² by Weigl Publishers Inc.
350 5th Avenue, 59th Floor
New York, NY 10118
Website: www.av2books.com www.weigl.com

Library of Congress Cataloging-in-Publication Data

McGill, Jordan.
Earth science fair projects / Jordan McGill.
p. cm. -- (Science fair projects)
Includes index.
ISBN 978-1-61690-651-1 (hardcover : alk. paper) -- ISBN 978-1-61690-655-9 (softcover : alk. paper) -- ISBN 978-1-61690-329-9 (online)
1. Earth sciences--Experiments--Juvenile literature. 2. Science--Methodology--Juvenile literature. 3. Science projects--Juvenile literature. 4. Science fairs--Juvenile literature. I. Title.
QE29.M355 2012
550.78--dc22
2011014123

Printed in the United States of America in North Mankato, Minnesota
2 3 4 5 6 7 8 9 0 15 14 13 12 11

Project Coordinator Jordan McGill
Art Director Terry Paulhus

092011
WEP230911

Every reasonable effort has been made to trace ownership and to obtain permission to reprint copyright material. The publishers would be pleased to have any errors or omissions brought to their attention so that they may be corrected in subsequent printings.

Weigl acknowledges Getty Images as its primary image supplier for this title.

CONTENTS

Take Part in a Science Fair

WHAT IS A SCIENCE FAIR?

A science fair is an event where students use the **scientific method** to create projects. These projects are then presented to spectators. Judges examine each project and award prizes for following the scientific method and preparing detailed displays. Some science fair winners move on to compete at larger fairs.

WHY SHOULD YOU TAKE PART IN A SCIENCE FAIR?

Science fairs are an excellent way to learn about topics that interest you. Winning is not the only reason to compete at a science fair. Science fairs are an opportunity for you to work hard on a project and show it off. You will also get to see the projects other students are presenting and learn from them as well.

WHERE DO I FIND A SCIENCE FAIR?

There are many fairs around the country and worldwide. Ask your teacher if he or she knows if any science fairs are held in your city. Once you find a fair to compete in, you can start preparing your project.

ANYTHING ELSE I SHOULD KNOW?

Before you start, you should begin a logbook. A logbook is a handwritten diary of the tasks you performed to complete your science fair project. Include any problems or interesting events that occur.

STEP 1
Select a topic

o begin, you must elect a topic. hoose a topic that ou would like to earn about. That vay, working on he project will be exciting.

STEP 2
Form a question about your topic

Think of a question you have about your topic. You can ask, "How do volcanoes erupt?" Another question could be, "How do fossils form?"

STEP 3
Research your question

Visit a library, and go online to research your topic. Keep track of where you found your **sources** and who wrote them. Most of your time should be spent learning about your topic.

STEP 4
Think about the answer to your question

Form a **hypothesis** that may answer your question. The sentence, "A volcano erupts when a great deal of energy builds up inside the volcano" is a hypothesis.

STEP 5
lan an experiment to test your hypothesis

esign an **xperiment** that ou can repeat and hat has observable **eactions**. Make detailed plan of hat you will do in our experiment nd what materials ou will need. Also nclude what you vill be looking for hen you do our experiment.

STEP 6
Conduct your experiment and record data

Carry out your experiment, and carefully observe what happens. Take notes. Record **data** if you need to. If you have nothing to note or record, reconsider whether your experiment has observable reactions.

STEP 7
Draw conclusions from your data

Were your predictions right? Sometimes, your hypothesis will be proven wrong. That is fine. The goal is to find the truth, not to be correct. When wrong, scientists think of a new hypothesis and try again.

STEP 8
Prepare a report and display

Write a report that explains your project. Include the topic, question, materials, plan, predictions, data, and conclusion in your report. Create a display that you can show at the science fair.

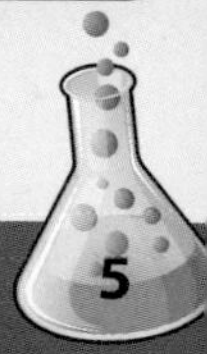

Picking an Earth Science Topic

Earth science is the study of Earth's origin, structure, and parts. Earth scientists look at rocks and minerals, earthquakes and volcanoes, and the processes that shape Earth's surface.

This book offers sample experiments for each of the six earth science topics listed below. These experiments can be used to develop a science fair project. Select a topic that interests you. Then, use the sample experiment in this book for your project. You can also think of your own experiment that fits the topic.

TOPIC 1 EARTHQUAKES

Earthquakes are sudden movements in the top layer of Earth. They happen along **faults** all over the world. Earthquakes can be destructive and dangerous. Scientists seek to find out what causes earthquakes and how they can be predicted.

TOPIC 2 FOSSILS

Fossils are **ancient** creatures or plants that have been pressed into the ground or rocks. Scientists who study fossils learn about Earth's past and the **organisms** that lived long ago.

TOPIC 3 MINERALS

Minerals are the building blocks of rocks on Earth and in space. Scientists examine minerals to classify them and to discover their origin.

TOPIC 4 ROCKS

From pebbles to boulders, rocks are found all over Earth. Scientists analyze rocks and mountains to learn what Earth is made from and how its landscapes are formed.

TOPIC 5 THE ROCK CYCLE

The rock cycle is the change of rocks from one type to another over time. The movement of rocks across the world is a product of the rock cycle. The movements that create earthquakes and build mountains are part of the rock cycle. Scientists study the rock cycle to find out how continents, mountains, and volcanoes form.

TOPIC 6 VOLCANOES

Volcanoes are openings on Earth's surface that sometimes spew **magma** and gas. Scientists watch volcanoes to learn why they erupt and to predict their **eruptions**.

How Do Seismographs Work?

Background Information

Earthquakes occur when rocks along a crack in Earth's surface suddenly shift. An earthquake is easily identified by shaking or trembling ground.

Most earthquakes are too small for people to feel, but some are bigger. Earthquakes can cause buildings to fall, roads to crack, and water dams to burst. Earthquakes cannot be prevented. Scientists try to find ways to predict where and when future earthquakes may occur so that people can prepare properly.

EXPERIMENT

Scientists use special instruments to measure changes in Earth. One tool is the seismograph. A seismograph measures and records vibrations on the ground and inside Earth. These measurements appear as wavy lines on paper. The lines record how Earth's crust is moving. Computerized seismographs allow seismologists to track earthquakes to within 6 miles (10 kilometers) of the **epicenter**. You can make your own seismograph using the following steps.

TIP #1
The more the box is shaking as you pull the paper through, the wider the curves of the line will be.

TIP #2
Add or remove weight from the cup to affect the line. Try jumping near the table or talking into the box instead of shaking it. Note how the line is affected.

Make a Seismograph in 7 Steps

CAUTION

Sharp Sticky

DIFFICULTY

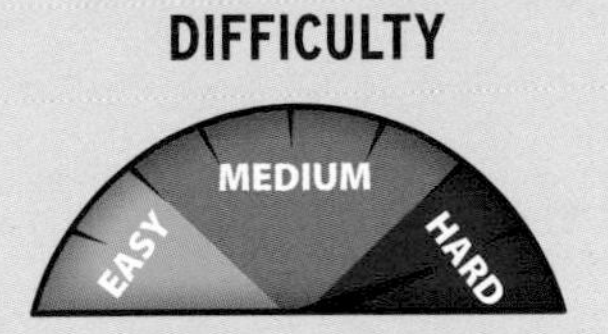

TIME 60 minutes

MATERIALS

- Plain white paper
- Scissors
- Tape or glue
- Fine point permanent marker
- String
- One plastic cup
- One large cardboard box
- One cup of rocks or marbles

INSTRUCTIONS

STEP 1 Cut the flaps off the box. Then, place the box in front of you with the opening on top.

STEP 2 Cut two small holes about 3 inches (7.6 centimeters) apart. The holes should be 1 inch (2.5 cm) from the top of the box's back wall.

STEP 3 Cut a wide hole at the bottom of the box. This hole should be under the two holes you cut in the last step. It should be wide enough to allow one piece of paper to pass through.

STEP 4 Cut a small hole in the bottom of the plastic cup. Place the marker through the hole so that the writing end sticks out the bottom. Use tape or glue to secure the marker. Then, cut two small holes near the top of the cup, one on each side.

STEP 5 Fill the cup half full with rocks or marbles.

STEP 6 Thread the string through the two holes in the top of the cup. Tie the string through the two holes in the back of the box. The cup should hang so that the marker just barely touches the bottom of the box. The cup should swing freely and mark the bottom of the box.

STEP 7 Place a piece of paper under the marker. Pull the paper through the hole in the back of the box slowly while someone shakes the box. What happens?

How Do Fossils Form?

Background Information

Fossils are the rocklike remains of ancient animals and plants. A fossil can be a hard part of an animal, such as a shell or a tooth. It can also be a footprint left behind in the mud. Fossils are usually found in layered rock called sedimentary rock. The layers of this type of rock form over time. Deeper layers contain material from an earlier age.

Fossils can be found in other materials as well. Millions of years ago, sticky resin oozed from pine tree stems, just as it does today. Sometimes, an insect or plant seed became stuck in the resin. Over time, the resin hardened and became another type of fossil called **amber**.

EXPERIMENT

TIP #1
You can use almost anything to make an imprint. Hand prints, toys, and sticks all work.

TIP #2
Make several fossils at a time in case some break.

Some fossils are formed when remains fall in soft mud. The mud dries over and around the remains. The remains eventually break apart, but an imprint remains. Scientists study these imprints to learn more about the organism that caused it. You can make your own fossil imprint using the following steps.

Form a Fossil in 6 Steps

CAUTION

Messy

DIFFICULTY

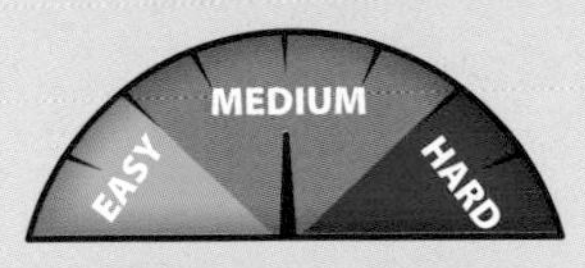

TIME 30 minutes

MATERIALS
- One large bowl
- 1 cup of flour
- 1/2 cup of salt
- 1 cup of brewed cold coffee
- Leftover grounds from brewed coffee
- Aluminum or wax paper
- Leaves, shells, or rocks

INSTRUCTIONS

STEP 1 With an adult's help, brew 1 cup of coffee. Be sure to keep the leftover coffee grounds from the filter.

STEP 2 Pour the flour, salt, brewed coffee, and the leftover coffee grounds into the bowl. Mix the ingredients together. Let the mixture sit for a few minutes until it sticks together like bread dough.

STEP 3 Take the dough-like mixture from the bowl, and place it on a piece of aluminum or wax paper. Squeeze and roll the dough with your hands until it is smooth.

STEP 4 Take a piece from the dough, and roll it into a ball. Flatten the piece with your hand.

STEP 5 Take the object you would like to use to make your fossil, and press it into the flattened piece. Let the flattened piece dry overnight with the object in it.

STEP 6 In the morning, carefully remove the object from the flattened piece. A dry cast should remain. This **cast** is similar to the impressions left in soft mud millions of years ago. What can you tell about the object by looking at the cast?

How Do Crystals Grow?

Background Information

Minerals are solid materials that are found in the natural environment. They are made of materials that were never alive. Minerals are all around us. The salt we put on food is a mineral. The sand on beaches is a mineral. Cars, buses, and bicycles are made of minerals. There are even minerals in our bodies. Minerals are one of the most common materials on Earth.

Some minerals are rare and expensive. They are called gemstones. Gemstones are usually shaped, polished, and placed in jewelry. Diamonds, for example, are often used in wedding rings and expensive jewelry.

EXPERIMENT

Look at grains of sand, salt, or sugar using a magnifying glass. You will see that they are made up of tiny parts. Minerals can sometimes grow into larger shapes called mineral crystals. Most crystals take hundreds or even thousands of years to grow, but some grow quite fast. Follow the steps below to grow sugar crystals.

TIP #1
Salt crystals can also be grown in much the same way. You could create a project that compares salt crystals and sugar crystals.

TIP #2
Be sure to document each step of this experiment with pictures or drawings. The crystals take time to grow. What does the experiment look like after sitting for one day? Two? Four? Keep track.

Grow Crystals in 5 Steps

CAUTION

Messy

Wet

DIFFICULTY

TIME 30 minutes + 1 week of observation

MATERIALS

- Two cups of sugar
- One cup of water
- Pan
- Glass jar
- Clothespin
- Cotton or wool string
- Paperclip

INSTRUCTIONS

STEP 1 Pour the water and sugar into the pan.

STEP 2 With an adult's help, boil the water and sugar mixture. Stir the mixture as it boils until the sugar is completely **dissolved**.

STEP 3 Pour the mixture into the glass jar. Fill the jar 3/4 full.

STEP 4 Tie the paperclip to one end of the string to provide weight. Place that end in the mixture. Take the clothespin, and clamp the other end of the string to the side of the jar. Make sure that the string does not fall completely into the mixture.

STEP 5 Wait four to seven days for the crystals to form. How big is the crystal after one week? What shape did it take on? Why do you think it grew in this way?

How Do Geologists Classify Rocks?

Background Information

The study of Earth's structure is called geology. Geologists are scientists who study rocks, mountains, and cliffs to learn what Earth is made from. They also learn how Earth has changed over time.

Geologists group rocks into three main types. These groups are based on how rocks form. Igneous rocks are made when magma cools. Sedimentary rocks are formed when layers of **sediment** become stuck together. Sedimentary rock is fragile. It is easily broken down by wind and rain. Heat and pressure cause sedimentary and igneous rocks to change. When they do this, a new type of rock, called metamorphic rock, forms.

EXPERIMENT

Much of Earth is made up of rock. Rocks are found at the bottoms of rivers and lakes. They are also found on mountain peaks. Rocks even form Earth's crust. Geologists use special methods to classify rocks. You can find many types of rocks in your own neighborhood. Take a walk, and try to find rocks that look different from each other. Use the steps on the next page to decide what kinds of rocks you have found.

TIP #1
The more places you look, the more types of rocks you will find. With an adult, try looking underground or near water.

TIP #2
Instead of collecting single rocks, you can make small containers for each type of rock and keep more than one sample. Glue the container to the box instead of a single rock.

Classify Rocks in 5 Steps

CAUTION

Messy

Sticky

DIFFICULTY

TIME 90 minutes

MATERIALS
- Rocks
- Glue
- Box

INSTRUCTIONS

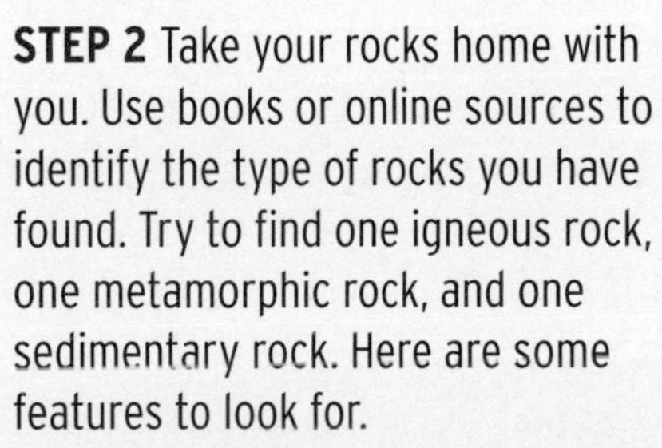

STEP 1 With an adult, walk around your house and neighborhood. Collect any interesting rocks that you find. Try to find rocks of different size, color, and appearance.

STEP 2 Take your rocks home with you. Use books or online sources to identify the type of rocks you have found. Try to find one igneous rock, one metamorphic rock, and one sedimentary rock. Here are some features to look for.
- Igneous rocks have small particles that look like crystals. They are often dense, or heavy.
- Metamorphic rocks feature lines of mineral grains that look like rocky stripes.
- Sedimentary rocks feel sandy to touch when rubbed because they are made of small particles. They should look layered from the side. If it is limestone, vinegar will make it bubble.

STEP 3 Prepare a box that has a place for every type of rock you found. Create a label for each type of rock.

STEP 4 Glue each rock to the box. Be sure to place each rock near its label.

STEP 5 Prepare a list of features that helped you identify each rock.

How Do Boulders Become Pebbles?

Background Information

Rocks on Earth's surface are exposed to sunshine, rain, ice, and heat. Over time, these elements slowly cause rocks to break down. This is called weathering.

Weathering can occur in a variety of ways. Temperature changes cause all objects, including rocks, to become slightly smaller or larger. With a rock, this can happen when water gets into cracks inside the rock. If the water freezes and then melts, the rock can break into smaller pieces.

Any of the three types of rock can be weathered. Water and temperature can break igneous, sedimentary, or metamorphic rock into sediment.

EXPERIMENT

Explore the effects of hot and cold temperatures on rocks. Different types of weathering can be imitated using rocks and household appliances. Follow these steps to explore how rocks break into smaller pieces.

TIP #1
You could also examine what happens when rocks are subjected to hot temperatures and then cold temperatures without a break in between. Is the weathering more severe when the temperature varies more quickly?

Explore Weathering in 5 Steps

TIP #2
Think of other forms of weathering that can be simulated at home. These could be added to your project.

CAUTION

Messy Adult's Help Wet

DIFFICULTY

TIME 60 minutes + 1 week of observation

MATERIALS

- Rocks
- Water
- A freezer or ice box
- An oven
- A pan or plate
- Sealable plastic bag
- One container or bowl

INSTRUCTIONS

STEP 1 With an adult, walk around your house and neighborhood. Collect at least two rocks that are about the same size and that look similar. Try to find rocks that are as close to each other as possible so you can examine how different types of weathering affect them.

STEP 2 At home, fill the bowl 3/4 full with water. Place one of the rocks in the bowl. Let it sit overnight.

STEP 3 Remove the rock from the water, and place it in a plastic bag. Take the other rock, and place it in a different plastic bag. Put both plastic bags in your freezer or ice box. Let them sit for at least 48 hours.

STEP 4 With an adult's help, preheat the oven to 450° F (232° Celsius). Put the rocks in the oven, and leave them there for at least 6 hours.

STEP 5 Place the rocks side by side, and record your observations. Did the rocks break apart? Did one rock break into more pieces than the other? How big were the pieces that broke off? The two types of weathering should have affected the rocks differently. Record the ways in which the rocks were affected. Performing the experiment several times with different rocks will give better results.

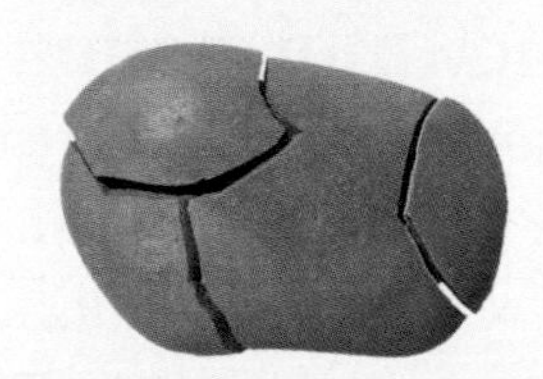

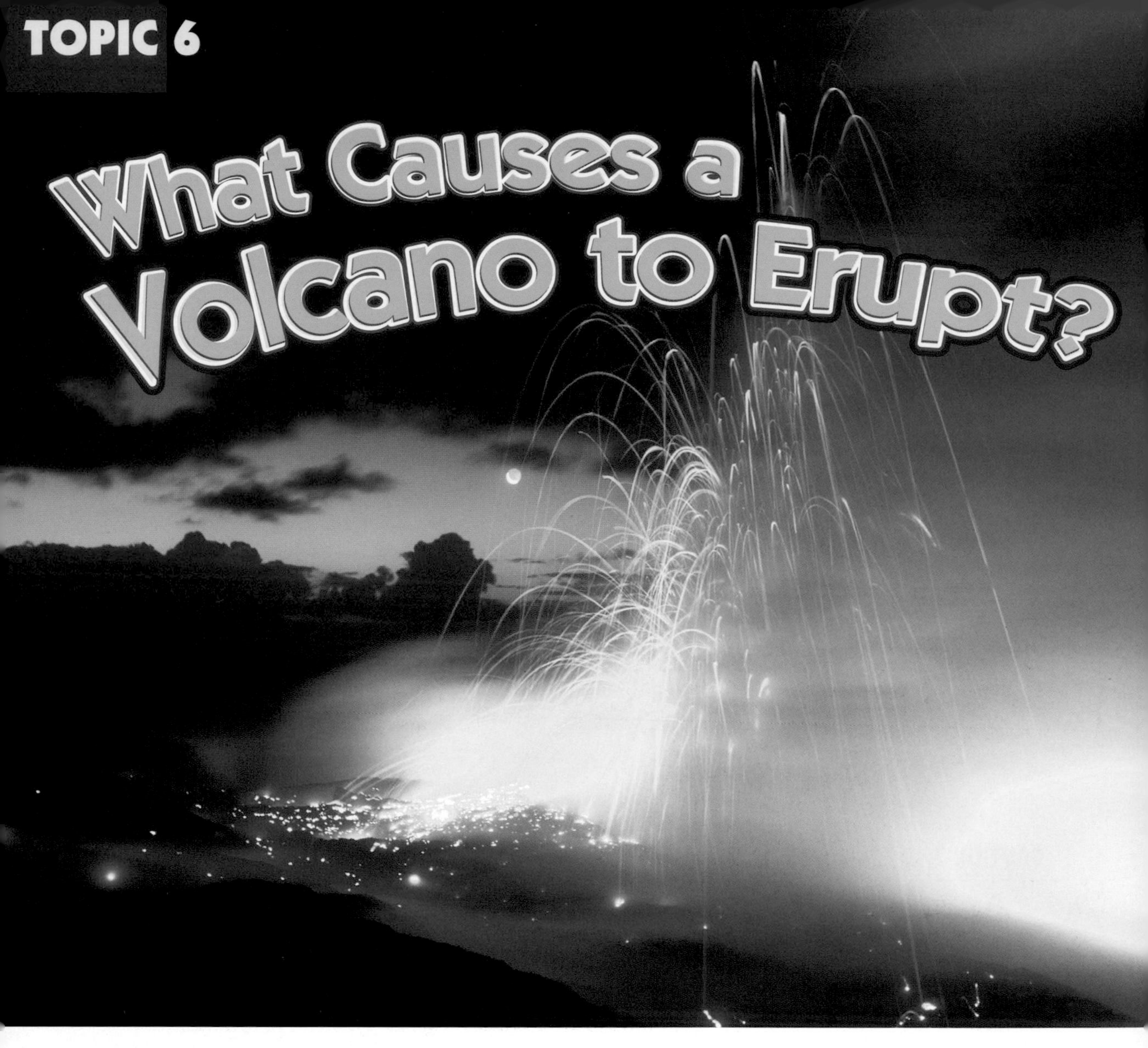

What Causes a Volcano to Erupt?

Background Information

A volcano is an opening in Earth's surface. This opening is sometimes the scene of a volcanic eruption. Eruptions occur when the gases and magma deep below Earth's surface mix together. The gases make the magma light enough to rise to Earth's surface. The magma collects in the chamber under a volcano. As more and more magma enters the chamber, pressure builds.

The magma eventually bursts through Earth's surface. The more gas there is in the magma, the more violent the eruption. Magma that reaches Earth's surface through the crater is called **lava**.

EXPERIMENT

You can simulate a volcanic eruption using items found in your house. This project is safe, but it can get messy. In this project, you will build a model of a volcano and create a chemical reaction to make it erupt. During the reaction, carbon dioxide gas will be produced. Real volcanoes produce carbon dioxide gas as well.

TIP #1
When preparing your report and display on this project, be sure to include how the reaction works and why this model accurately mirrors a real volcanic eruption.

TIP #2
Changing the amount of any substance used in the project will affect the size of the eruption.

Create a Volcano in 6 Steps

CAUTION

Messy Toxic Sticky

DIFFICULTY

EASY MEDIUM HARD

TIME 40 minutes

MATERIALS
- Modeling clay
- White glue
- 1 inch (2.5 cm) deep baking tray or other pan
- One plastic bottle
- Warm water
- Baking soda
- Red and yellow food coloring
- Dishwashing liquid
- Vinegar

INSTRUCTIONS

STEP 1 Glue the plastic bottle to the bottom of the tray or pan. Then, cover the plastic bottle with the modeling clay. Shape the clay to make it look like a volcano. Spread the clay onto the bottom of the pan to make the model more realistic.

STEP 2 Fill the bottle 3/4 full with warm water.

STEP 3 Add three to four squirts of red and yellow food coloring to the water.

STEP 4 Put three to four drops of dishwashing liquid into the water and food coloring mixture.

STEP 5 Add 3 to 4 tablespoons of baking soda to the mixture.

STEP 6 Before you carry out this step, get ready to step back. Pour 1/2 cup of vinegar into the volcano, and watch it erupt. When the vinegar is added, a reaction occurs between it and the baking soda. Energy builds until it is too great to be contained inside the volcano.

Preparing Your Report

Once your experiment is completed, write a report. The purpose of the report is to summarize your work. You want others to understand the question, the research, and the experiment. The report also explains your results and ties everything together in a conclusion.

1 **Title**
The title of your report should be the question you are trying to answer.

2 **Purpose**
This section of the report should include a few sentences explaining why you chose this project.

3 **Hypothesis**
The hypothesis is made up of one sentence that explains the answer your experiment was meant to prove.

4 **Background**
Write a summary of the information you found during your research. You most likely will not need to use all of your research.

5 **Materials**
Write a list of the materials you used during your experiment. This is the same as the list of materials included with each sample experiment in this book.

6 **Plan**
Write out the steps needed to carry out your experiment.

7 **Results**
Write all observations and relevant data you recorded during your experiment here. Include any tables or graphs you made.

8 **Conclusion**
In this part of the report, state what you learned. Be sure to write how you think your results prove or disprove your hypothesis. You should also write your hypothesis again somewhere in this section. It is acceptable if your hypothesis was false. What is important is that you were creative and followed the scientific method.

9 **Bibliography**
Include an alphabetical list by the author's last name of all sources you used.

Making Your Display

Most science fairs encourage the use of a backboard to display your project. Most displays use a three-panel backboard. It stands up on its own and is easy to view.

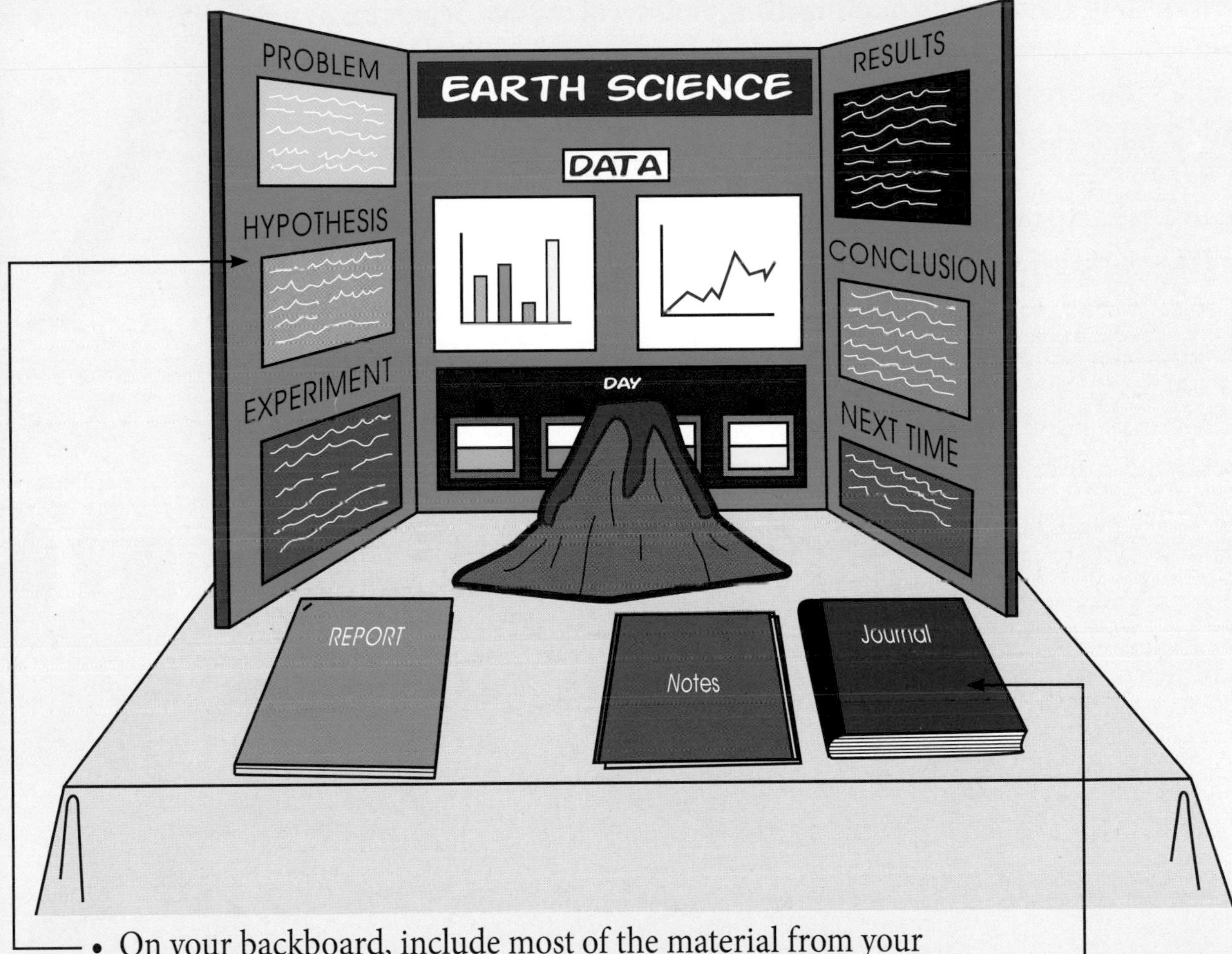

- On your backboard, include most of the material from your report. Leave out the background information. You may also include photos or drawings to help explain your project.

- Most often, your backboard will be placed on a table. On the table, you can include any models you created or samples you collected. Also include the logbook and a copy of your report.

- If possible, you may also perform your experiment at the fair.

Impressing the Judges

Know the Rules

Judges expect that you know the rules. Breaking rules can lead to lost points and even **disqualification**. Rules will change depending on who is organizing the science fair. Before you begin your project, talk to the organizers of the fair you plan to compete in. Ask them for a list of rules.

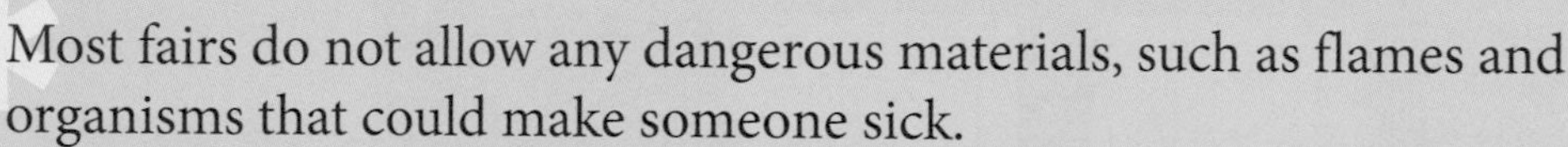

Most fairs do not allow any dangerous materials, such as flames and organisms that could make someone sick.

Practice Presenting

To stand out at the science fair, you have to give a strong presentation to the judges. Write a short speech that covers what you want to say. Your speech should summarize why you chose the project. It should also explain the experiment and your conclusions. Practice this speech until you are comfortable. Speak confidently and clearly.

Many judges will ask questions. Present your project to friends and family. Then, have them ask questions as if they were judges.

Dress For an Event

A science fair is a special event. It is different from an ordinary day. When you go somewhere special, do your parents have you dress up? Judges look at every part of your presentation, including you. Wear something special. Comb your hair. Tuck in your shirt. Tie your shoes. You are presenting yourself as much as your project.

amber: hard, see-through substance that came from extinct trees; a type of fossil
ancient: very old
cast: a mold
classify: to organize according to class or category
data: items of information
disqualification: to be eliminated from a competition
dissolved: to completely mix with a liquid
epicenter: the point of Earth's surface directly above the focus of an earthquake
eruptions: ejections of gas, steam, ash, or lava with great force
experiment: a test, trial, or procedure
faults: breaks in rock formations
hypothesis: a possible explanation for a scientific question
lava: the molten, fluid rock that issues from a volcano
magma: the molten rock material under Earth's crust
organisms: any living things
reactions: when two or more substances combine to make a new chemical substance
scientific method: a system of observation
sediment: solid pieces of material that come from the weathering of rock
sources: the books or websites from which research was obtained

Log on to www.av2books.com

AV² by Weigl brings you media enhanced books that support active learning. Go to www.av2books.com, and enter the special code found on page 2 of this book. You will gain access to enriched and enhanced content that supplements and complements this book. Content includes video, audio, web links, quizzes, a slide show, and activities.

Audio
Listen to sections of the book read aloud.

Video
Watch informative video clips.

Embedded Weblinks
Gain additional information for research.

Try This!
Complete activities and hands-on experiments.

WHAT'S ONLINE?

 Try This!	 Embedded Weblinks	 Video	EXTRA FEATURES
Create useful observation sheets. Make a judging sheet. Make a timeline to make sure projects are finished on time. Complete fun interactive earth science activities.	Check out more information about earth science topics. Learn how to coordinate a science fair. Learn more about creating an effective display.	Watch a video about earth science. Check out another video about earth science.	 **Audio** Listen to sections of the book read aloud.  **Key Words** Study vocabulary, and complete a matching word activity. 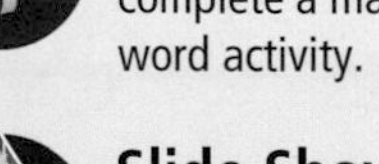 **Slide Show** View images and captions, and prepare a presentation  **Quizzes** Test your knowledge.

AV² was built to bridge the gap between print and digital. We encourage you to tell us what you like and what you want to see in the future.

Sign up to be an AV² Ambassador at www.av2books.com/ambassador.

Due to the dynamic nature of the Internet, some of the URLs and activities provided as part of AV² by Weigl may have changed or ceased to exist. AV² by Weigl accepts no responsibility for any such changes. All media enhanced books are regularly monitored to update addresses and sites in a timely manner. Contact AV² by Weigl at 1-866-649-3445 or av2books@weigl.com with any questions, comments, or feedback.